Relapse
&
Release

Antione Denzel Lacey

ISBN: 978-0-578-87585-9

LIFE LESSON

The fall is easy. It's the healing that makes it all difficult. I gave my heart to a dream that once was. Now, I'm left sweeping up the pieces of yesterday's broken memory.

CONTENTS

Relapse & Release

GRIEF

(noun) - Mental suffering or distress over affliction or loss.

When April Fools isn't a Joke

When she says,
I have something to tell you.
Your mind embraces the drop
And proceeds to get the parachute.

She says,
She wants to be alone.
Your mouth is dry.
Your thoughts are empty.

Your body pulls the parachute strings
Because the world you know is
Crashing before you...
Then,
 blackness.

My body hasn't felt the same
Since you left.
Cold,
As if time shattered its glass
And severed my heart.

You,
Was a part of me.
Empyreal thoughts about a future with you
Was swept away
With your gentle words.

Relapse & Release

You,
A presence dreamt of.
The muse to my writings,
Breathing truth about how I felt
In every line.

Now,
The shadows of our memories
Only exists in the ambiance
Of never more.

Sometimes,
I'll wake up
Thinking I'd heard the serenades
Of your voice.
A low whisper of
"Good morning King".

But…
Only to hear
The distant buzzing
Of my alarm
To get ready for work.

Depression

Depression is
A silent scream
In a room full of people.

Depression is
The backhand compliment of trying.
Being selfless;
Working on self-improvements,
But still gets abandoned.

Depression is
Saying you're not good enough.
You've met all the requirements
But still not hitting the bar.

Depression is
A bed you used to call home.
A house with vacant emptiness
With a "*we moved*" sign
In place of your heart.

Depression is
A gun sitting on your nightstand.
Hollow,
Waiting for your candy crush dreams
To play Russian Roulette.

Depression is
Red...

Denial

Teardrops stained my vision red
As your face pierced through
The cracks of my phone screen.
I ventured into our past,
Taking hikes through our old photos
In hopes of a better tomorrow.
I held your hand
As we walked through
Our dates in time.
Your voice,
A distorted memory
As the walk became endless.
Time wasn't against us,
Only the wind.

Day 3

I treat my bed as a safe zone.
It cuffs the shades of my window
And cascades me into my salvation.
My bed says good morning.

It sees my eyes drowned with discomfort.
My bed gives me a pillow.
The sun
 Beams upon my melanin.
I turn away as if I'm afraid to look at it.

My bed,
Sits in silence and looks at me.
It knows I'm scared
To face another morning
Of what my heart feels.

I drag myself to the mirror.
Emanating my feelings
Into my reflection.
My fears became the titanic ship of worries
Washed down the sink.

My bed calls for me.
I ponder back,
Pulling back the labia
And driving into the womb.

Relapse & Release

It's my haven until tomorrow.
Until
Dawn groans my name
Again to wake up.

3 AM

How can I let the dead sleep?
When my mind is constantly
Resurrecting the memories
Of a walking corpse.

I...
Keep dreaming of *you.*
Every time I think of you
My Frankenstein disembowel the stitches
Of its own heart
And hands it to you.

As an offering.
A sacrifice.
Awestruck with the thought
The lightning bolts
Of this storm
Can create another heartbeat.

5 AM

I sit in the darkness.
I listen to my heart's greatest hits
As it slow dances
With my brain
On the checked dance floor.

There's blood on it.
My heart tries to keep up
with my brain,
But proceed to do the cha-cha slide.

My brain mimics the moves
But loses it.
My heart scrambles to clutch
Onto my brain's hands.

It's slippery wet.
Same as the floor.
Red.
Dripping with the aspirations
Of drying
In a new mood color.

My brain stops.
It smells the scent of pain.
It knows my heart is tired.
Tired of getting its feet stepped on
In this moment of movement.

Relapse & Release

I guess this is how my love is.
When my heart breaks a beat,
My brain can't process
In its own tune.
It can't move to the sounds
Of sorrow
When peace evacuates the room.

Mop water of scriptures
Only sink so deep
When time is in play
with red oozing through the cracks.

The blood,
Lying beneath the lines
Of fulfillment and companionship.

My heart,
Bloody and covered in bruises.
Grabs onto my brain
And says "let's try again."

Body

I apologize.
I'm sorry for using you
As a scapegoat
When things go wrong.

I tripped over the asphalts
I call feel my feelings.
My precious temple,
I know you need to heal.

You've worn our heart
On our sleeves for too long,
The blood splatters are starting
To look the same.

We can't blame the past
On the present
If we're trying to grow.

I know you're in pain.
I know you're in pain...
I know you're trying to tunnel
Through the pain,
But body just rest.

Heal.
I weep for you
In the hours of the night.
I hope these Lazarus tears
Can heal you.

Relapse & Release

If this heartache doesn't kill you
Just please,
Live for us...

Process

Healing feels like
Performing surgery on your own heart
With no anesthetics.
The agonizing screams
Your mind makes when it's alone
In a room full of souls
And still,
Be seen as the elephant.

Wishing well [His Pain]

I wish
Cupid would stop fucking with me.
Every time I give my heart
To someone
They devalued the sticker price.

I wish
You didn't departmentalize
My existence
Into file 13.

I wish
The stars on your Orion's belt
Were better aligned than the big dipper
In our constellation.

I wish
I wasn't another casualty
Engulfed in your Charlotte's web.

I wish
The only thing that changed
Between us was time.

I wish...
I wish I were enough for you.
I wish love didn't hurt so much.
I wish these nightmares didn't become
A trojan horse into this temple.

Wishful Thinking

I hope you've cherished
Our memories like unforgotten prayers
And not allow it
To become a wilted up dandelion
In the wind.

Skips

If I could rewind time,
I would go back to the moment
Where our eyes locked on
Over a bowl of conversation and fried rice.

Back when we kissed beneath the depths
And darkness of movie chatter.
Where the phrase "what took you so long?"
Would alternate throughout my mind.

I would,
Two-step in the blissful moments
Of our late-night talks
And wake up seeing myself
Looking at you in a peaceful slumber.

I would venture through
The times when we explored
Each other's temples.
You were Lora Croft and I Indiana Jones.
We analyzed our consciousness
In the treasured keepsakes of our back seats.

Take me back when
We whispered our goals
Into existence.
We dominated the game like dominoes.
We were seeking God
In more ways than one.
I felt good in your company.

Relapse & Release

Sometimes,
I would pray for someone
Like you.
Us,
Living in this sandcastle
I'd built.

Possessing precious memories in it.
Only to see it
Slip away through my fingers
And washed away with the tide.

Nostalgic Memory

We constantly emerge.
Self-indulging ourselves in something
We call love.
The gift from God
With the aroma of amnesia.

I've met you somewhere
I think…
I dreamt about you through
These stanzas and metaphors
My mind continues to produce.

Our first glance
Was when these words dropped
From a place of privacy.

When you're near,
I get these butterflies
Neither Jill Scott
Or Micheal Jackson can predict.

In the midst of passion,
You guided these hand away
From your keepsake.
Intertwining my fingers with yours
Keeping them tamed.

Sometimes,
I asked myself who've sent
Your grace.
I know things happen for a reason
And patience is a virtue.

Relapse & Release

You were a companion
To my shadows.
Someone who ignited my confidence
When doubtful silence
Clouded my mind.
For this,
I am grateful.

Timing

She saw him
In a nostalgic room
As his poetic words
Flowed over rhythmic snaps.
He wrote her
Into his existence.
She was searching
For the king within the man.
While
He was searching for himself
Trying to be the *"MAN"*
For her.

Seasons

You can't cage a bird,
Who has grown its wings.
If its heart yearns for the land,
It'll fly back.

Goodbye My Beloved

I've never been good at goodbyes.
I've always welcomed hellos
And genuine smiles
Like my life depended on it.

Then,
There was you.
A gentle gaze of sunshine
I dreamt about
Before our names were brought into existence.

You were...
A melaninaided songbird
Who prayed for a brighter today.
I never wanted you
To drift away into the arms
Of another miscellaneous person.

I never wanted you to think
I was less than what
I was giving.
Even if I was learning
To love bits of myself.

I've felt the seasons change
When your mind
Left the place
My heart resonated as a home.

Relapse & Release

Here,
I bury the reminders of forever no more.
I accept our fate
As grains of sand from which we came.
Now I know.
Eventually,
Longevity has its own expiration date
When the heart stops believing
Its own story.

For Your Eyes Only

To whom it may concern.
I don't know who you are
Or when we shall meet.
I'll do my best to hold
God's lien cloth over my eyes
And let faith lead the way.

I want you to show me.
Show me how to love you
Beyond my understanding
When words don't fall
Upon my ears.

If my eyes can see
The glittery golden brownstones
Of heavens gates.
I won't hesitate
To ask for your hand.

I will not dangle
Harmonious carrots in your face
And lead you down a path
Of nothingness.

I will give you all that I have
But,
Just don't waste my time.

Don't waste seconds
Contemplating about a future
With me
If your third eye
Don't see the bigger picture.

Relapse & Release

Don't take my kindness
For weakness
If my tone doesn't
Roar like a prideful lion.

Just know that
I'm **HIM**.
Him that dives into
The depth of your soul
And claiming your heart
As mines.

So,
Whoever you may be
I'm waiting
for you...

I Pray This Love

I pray that my love is
Like this poem.
A beautiful masterpiece without a sad ending.
A road to a new beginning
Painted with hieroglyphics and a song
meant for ages.

I pray this love is the smell of Sunday mornings,
Easily cracked eggs
with melaninaded OJ
And the golden sounds of Jill Scott
Playing in the background.

I pray this love
Is bound by happiness
and joy.

I pray this love is rooted.
If we touch,
Our hearts would be in sync type love.

I pray this love is like a negro spiritual.
If I get lost
This love will help me
navigate back to you.

I pray this love would last
Like sticks of gum
On a hot day.

I pray this love
Is like God listening to my heart's
Greatest hits on his iPhone.
Jamming to every beat
And the pulse of my soul
Trying to reach **HER.**

My love.
Mi Amor.
I love you.
That is all…

This Poem

This poem is nice.
This poem has the backbone
That can break open
The gates of Olympus.

This poem is kind.
This poem is mesmerized by nature
And wisdom.

This poem has a little kick to it
Like the kickback bass of a drum,
Or the spice in Louisiana gumbo.

This poem is love.
The crippling notion
Of being broken into pieces,
Sweep that up.

This poem is healing.
Fixing itself back into understandable
Stanzas and metaphors.
Whether it's rehearsing a final goodbye
Or singing melaninaided songs.

This poem has a journey.
A milestone with a few potholes,
Only time can fix.

This poem is giving...
This poem is filled with joy.
This poem is welcoming with open arms...
This poem is release.
Ejaculation at its finest.

Relapse & Release

This poem is a beat.
The beating sound of a heart
From a distant land,
The soul yearns for.

This poem is a man
Still searching for God within
His temple.
This poem is *I*,
And *I* this poem.

I've been looking for God
In the blankness of my temple.
I've gambled with my heart
So many times,
The books weren't in my favor.

I reached into my pockets
And pulled out bloody mustard seeds.
Somehow,
This poem has faith.

Somehow,
This poem believes
It has no end
Only just a beginning.

Prayer

I ask God to Forgive me.
Forgive me
If my fears discard the life raft of love
When you tried to rescue me.
When the waters of my anxiety
Gotten to my neck.

I forgot your words
Telling me to stay and be still
When the waters aren't that deep.
Forgive me for surrendering to the vices
And relapsing on my pain.

I've drunk my spill.
I've downed the bottles of my urges
And the bodies of reminiscing
Doesn't seem to get any better.

Please show me how.
How can I give you my fears
When the bag always refilling itself.
It shovels its way back into my thoughts
Until I lose again.

My battles,
A war I wage against myself when my reality
Scar knuckle dragged me into a black hole.
Sometimes,
I feel like these battles go on
And the war isn't reconciled.

Relapse & Release

I ask that you forgive me.
When I go too far into the abyss,
Please guide me.
All I have is mustard seeds in my pockets
And a fragile heart of hope.

Today

Today,
I finally learned how to breathe.
I've taken my first breaths
Into a righteous perspective.
I gave myself time
To analyze the depths
Of life's confusion.

Today,
I took a grasp on greatness
And put my foot
In the back of my depression
Ass.
I AM FUCKING AMAZING.

Today,
I'm learning this time
I needed time
To grow and manifest
Into the man
I was destined to be.

Today,
I am ENOUGH.
Today,
I am LOVED.
Today,
My greatness is beyond measure.

Today,
I am more.

Letter to Self

Dear Self,
Take this time to breathe.
There's no need to beat yourself up
Over situations
That vacated your existence.

You are more than enough.
You don't have to prove your worth
To anyone who doesn't
Treasure your soul.

You are a loveable person
Who is deserving of the love you give.
The kindred spirit who won't
Give up.

You are not someone's trial service,
Nor the bottom-shelf product that's
Easy to come by.
Neither does your spirit
Equate to being a secondary option.

The path your on is greater
Than the fears of the unknown.
Trust in it
Like the hand of God guiding
you through.

You got this...

Acceptance [Letting Go]

One day,
The feeling of agony
Will meet its demise with a smile.
You will no longer wake up
To it nipping at your feet.
Your mornings will
Feel like pleasant welcomes
Kissing the air.
Your bed,
Won't remain a casket
Only a place to rest
Because you need it.
Your tears will be a journey of stories
Told to your future self
As you survived the fall.
Soon,
You will start believing your **own** words
Until you can cut them
Into spades
And have winnable books.

www.ingramcontent.com/pod-product-compliance
Lightning Source LLC
Chambersburg PA
CBHW060429090426
42734CB00011B/2501